FUTURE
TERRIFIC

PLANNING CHANGE IN MIDLIFE

FUTURE
TERRIFIC

PLANNING CHANGE IN MIDLIFE

Judi Striano, Ph.D.

PROFESSIONAL PRESS
P.O. Box 50343
Santa Barbara, California 93150

FUTURE TERRIFIC: PLANNING CHANGE IN MIDLIFE. COPYRIGHT © 1988 by Judi Striano. All rights reserved. Printed in the United States of America. No part of this book may be used or reproduced in any manner without written permission except for brief quotations in critical articles and reviews. For information write to Professional Press, P.O. Box 50343, Santa Barbara, California 93150.

Library of Congress
Cataloging-in-Publication Data

Striano, Judi Cecere, 1941-
    Future Terrific: Planning Change in Midlife
FIRST EDITION
        p.   cm.
    Bibliography: p.
    ISBN 0-943659-05-1 $7.95
    1. Midlife crisis.   I. Title
BF724.65.M53S77   1989
155.6--dc 19   89-3816
                                        CIP

Contents

The story of the
Midcareer Development Institute   13

Chapter 1

The Vision   19

Chapter 2

Lifecycle Changes   45

Chapter 3

Who Am I?   65

Chapter 4

Plans, Action Steps, Time Lines   *85*

Clinical psychologist Dr. Judi Striano has worked as a psychotherapist for twenty years, is author of books and articles about psychotherapy, currently lives in New York City and Santa Barbara, California, and is introducing this first book on a new approach to midlife transition and lifelong self-renewal.

Dedicated to

Frederic M. Hudson, Ph.D.

Management and psychology graduate school
Founding President,
college professor, ordained minister, and
Founder and President of the
Midcareer Development Institute

Frederic M. Hudson, Ph.D. founded the Midcareer Development Institute in 1987. With a 100 member faculty located in most major cities, MDI serves clients throughout the United States. Dr. Hudson leads training seminars for individuals, corporations, and educational institutions on life planning, leadership development, transition management, career renewal, and creative retirement planning.

MIDCAREER DEVELOPMENT INSTITUTE
3463 State Street
Suite 520
Santa Barbara, California 93105
(805) 682-3883

The Story of MDI

This is the story of

the Midcareer Development Institute (MDI) in Santa Barbara, California, an organization devoted to helping adults in midlife manage transitions, personal and professional change, and the launching of their lives in new directions.

I was in midlife and wanting a career change. But no one else wanted this for me. To "common sense" friends it was impractical. I had a "good" job with enviable prestige and a high salary that allowed me to live well, especially for a single woman without the double income of a couple.

Although I had wanted to be a psychologist ever since my early teen years, enjoyed my profession, and wanted to continue in it, I had had a much earlier dream, from as far back as I could remember, of being a journalist, and wanted to try that as a professional also. As a child of seven I would write poems about robins and Springtime and all else in nature that thrilled me. But non-stop schooling, all the way through a Ph.D. in clinical psychology, had narrowed my gushing river of creative expression to the rigorous academically focused writing required to get my degrees and licenses.

FUTURE TERRIFIC

Now that I was accomplished professionally and financially independent, the little girl's poetry was with me more and more. And now that I was politically sophisticated with a strong social conscience, I saw much on my planet that I wanted to change, that I wanted to write about—from social injustice to the hope-bearing robin appearing as the first sign of Spring after the long dreary winter. I had a lot to say.

Luckily for me I had MDI. Its founder, Dr. Frederic Hudson, didn't think I was abnormal. Didn't think I needed psychotherapy to help me "adjust" to being a "stable adult" who wouldn't have such fanciful flights. He believed I was of "sound mind," and that if I believed that was what I needed, then that was what I needed. And he stood by me, affirming my revival. Endorsing the parts of me that were re-surfacing. Accepting my new life design. All this cautiously, to be sure I was being practical enough so I wouldn't burn my bridges back to any part of my life that I wanted to keep or go back to at any time. And still earn a living, of course.

With new energy and my joint new direction—to be both a psychologist and a writer—I decided to write about the experience which had been so transformative for me. I want other midlife new-path-seekers to be encouraged, to be guided by

14

The Story of MDI

their dreams, to follow their feelings, to know it's all right, not to deny what they need to fulfill their potentials.

This is the story of MDI.

Judi Striano, Ph.D.

CHAPTER 1

The Vision

The Vision

CHAPTER 1

The Vision

For all of them, suddenly it was closer to the end than it was to the beginning, and death had definable features, as actor Bill Holden said in the movie "Network." They were counting time left to live rather than years since birth. It was the dark night of the soul.

Reviewing the memorabilia of their lives, some of their teenage dreams had been lost along the way to "making it" in the adult world. What they had was no longer, or never had been, what they wanted.

FUTURE TERRIFIC

Mark, a 41 year old computer engineer with a Ph.D. from MIT lamented that he seemed to have "forgotten to get married," sidestepping the intimacy that is so much the stuff of life, and also yearned to be a "starving artist." After struggling with objects and ideas all his life, he had belatedly and painfully discovered feelings.

A rich man, head of his own corporation, Jonathan thought that as the captain of the high school football team, conqueror of the Homecoming Queen, and inheritor of his father's business, he was headed for blissful perfection. But when the thrill of achievement in business became stale, and his daughter married and he and his wife were left alone with each other, he seemed for the first time to feel the distance in their relationship, and to know that his wife felt she was only vaguely outlined as an individual, and that he'd never given her the attention she needed.

Marty, a 45 year old international playboy living in his yacht in Santa Barbara paradise, felt hollow travelling the seas of the world, wanted to take a deep sea dive into more permanence and commitment, and thought it was time for him "to get a job."

The Vision

A vibrant and stunning blonde, having tossed away the glory of life in New York City as a successful attorney to marry a West Point graduate and live his military life for 25 years, Jean now wanted to leave the Colonel and pick up her career again.

Married at 17, telling her husband "I hope you know what we're doing, because I don't," after 40 years down the road and 3,000 miles across the country a "housewife," Nancy, joked "I ruined my life and had a happy marriage;" but her enormous comic talent was bursting for an audience, and her identity wanted recognition for something other than as a wife and mother.

Ann was 67. Her husband left her and their three daughters thirty years ago. She had worked as a secretary in a civil service job since then, supporting her children and paying off the mortgage on her house. Her boss had been pressuring her to retire since she was 62; he wanted to hire someone younger. She told the group "I'm afraid to leave. I don't know what to do with myself. If I could feel excited about something else and want it enough, I would retire more easily. I'm scared, frustrated, anxious, have no energy."

All were in transition from one chapter of their lives to another, from one place to another on the

FUTURE TERRIFIC

journey around the circle of beginnings to endings to beginnings.

Travelling from all parts of the country to this hilltop in Santa Barbara, these diverse personalities introduced themselves in what was to be a five-day group workshop that they hoped would lead them, under the guidance of the Director of the Midcareer Development Institute (MDI), Dr. Frederic Hudson, to designing a new future at midlife.

Round and round we go, and where we stop nobody knows. Not this time. With a visionary's daydream and a businessman's action plan and time line, under careful supervision their destinies will be charted. Imagination and reason, fantasy and practicality, wishes and necessities will be negotiated.

"You've got to have a dream. If you don't have a dream, how you gonna make a dream come true?" From "South Pacific," wasn't it? If you don't have a dream, you'll spend your life making someone else's dream come true.

"We hold these truths to be self-evident" said a founding father of our country Thomas Jefferson in the Declaration of Independence as he laid out the American Dream. "I have a dream," yearned Martin Luther King in the 1960s as he painted a picture of equality and fairness in America.

The Vision

If you don't know where you're going, you'll end up somewhere else, somewhere you may not want to be. "What do I want?" "Where am I going?" "Who's going with me?" Musts to wonder, musts to answer. How to know? An adolescent dreamer dreams many possibilities. How to get to the possibility of possibilities for this later go-around? Write a letter to your 17 year old self. As you're falling off to sleep tonight tell yourself you're going to dream some scenes of your future. A group guided imagery, part of the workshop experience, was enough to prompt most to envision.

Jonathan the rich man saw his painting on the wall of the Louvre, the Paris museum. Pure fantasy. He'll have to plan more realism in his artistry. He could design something utilitarian to sit in or ride in or to put to work for us. But he wanted his creations to be uplifting, to ring bells, to fly with his spirit.

"I saw myself," volunteered the housewife, Nancy, in a musical comedy on the Broadway stage." Ultimately she will aim for radio talk show host in Los Angeles. That would be reachable. Poet Robert Browning said "Ah, but a man's reach should exceed his grasp. Or what's a heaven for?" But, said the rich man, "You can't get so high in the sky on your dream that you jump out of the plane without knowing how to operate your parachute." He hoped that wouldn't happen because during this week he will have

FUTURE TERRIFIC

planned each step of the way in a road map of do-able tasks to follow to his goals.

Midlife adults must not give up their dreams. Dreaming is not just for the young. Fly to the moon, as Henry David Thoreau tells us; don't just build a woodshed.

> *"The youth gets together his materials to build a bridge to the moon, or, perchance, a palace or temple on the earth, and, at length, the middle-aged man concludes to build a wood-shed with them."*

To stop dreaming is to have stagnant images of your possibilities, to lose hope, to become lifeless. A dream is energy; you get a burst of energy every time you think of it. A dream feels as though it is pulling you toward it from without and pushing you toward it from within. Its pull is the perspective it gives on what's important in your life; its push is high level enthusiasm. You know you have a vision when it won't let you go, and others are attracted to it. You know you have a vision when it seems to be already guiding you toward making it a reality in your life, and you don't have to explain it perfectly to anyone. Dreams are how companies get born, Olympic races get won, music gets written, and inventions get made. When you have a vision, you have a mission. You know what you want.

The Vision

Your greatest power is your capacity to imagine, vision, dream, over and over and over again. It is part of the lifestyle of the self-renewing adult. More than any other simple human endeavor, your vision of the future is the key to your empowerment. Take your passion, and make it happen!

Take a journey into yourself to identify your future ahead. Position yourself to know yourself a little better, to face tough decisions, and discover new paths ahead. Envision a future that will provide your personal success. Write it out like a story, like a drama unfolding. Let your mind dance in every direction so you get a grasp on everything you want to happen. Give yourself permission to dream without constraints of money or time. Believe you have everything you need to actualize the dream. Picture yourself a year from now when you are living in the midst of your realized dream. You are your grand dream. In your imagination, drift away to a place where you always feel comfortable. Imagine that you've done exactly what you wanted to do. Everything has worked. The vision you had a year ago has come true. Look back and see what you've done in your life to make this happen. How will your life be the same and how will it be different? Where will you be? Who will be with you? What will you be doing? Work? Play? Leisure? Let your vision touch everything you want transformed. Create a dream

FUTURE TERRIFIC

that will make the next year a personal mission for you.

Treat the assignments of this week lightly, Dr. Hudson cautions, and they will do the same for you. Do them as an obligation, and they will politely serve you, a little. Pour yourself into them as if your life depended on them, and they will help you see yourself and your future with fresh insight, new decisions, and a deep possession of the path that is right for you. Ask deeper questions of yourself than you have ever asked.

Insofar as you wish, share your thoughts with the group you will be meeting with all week. If you choose, invite your group to join your quest for the right answers. The tasks of this week will be a catalyst for unleashing the wisdom of your peers.

If our exercises do not serve you, invent your own way to accomplish what we seek to do. Do not come up empty. The resources of this week are vast, and if our tasks do not light a torch to your journey, find your own torch and light it. Find your own ways to look at your dilemmas, to claim your strengths, to identify your unique options, and to map out your personal plan that gives a glow to your life with realism and success. Use this week for guiding your "self" with the future you truly want and deserve.

The Vision

Besides the experiential work in their group meetings, all are given a manual with paper and pencil exercises to coach them to pathfinding. This becomes a written journal, a diary, a record of their discoveries, notes of their internal dialogue with themselves...important for being alone with yourself and for privacy in your honesty. Maybe not all your secrets are to be shared so easily, or ever, with others. In the form of a personal strategy, it helps answer these questions: "Who are you? What are your strengths? What are your weaknesses? What are the stumbling blocks? Where are you going? What are your priorities? What is your vision, your mission?" The manual summarizes what academic researchers know about midlife adults. More information. More support.

In the past it was believed that development continued until age 16, or perhaps to 18, followed by a long plateau in which random things accrued, and at about 60 or 65 "aging" began. Now we know that we do not arrive at adulthood, we do not "grow up." We simply continue and change. Adulthood is not a noun; it is a verb. Transitions are normal. But we haven't been told that. A myth of our society is that when we're 20 or 25 we're supposed to be "grownup." We're supposed to be "together." We're supposed to be through adolescence. Well, adolescence is simply a transition—a major transition. Then there

FUTURE TERRIFIC

is "middlescence," and then later in our lives it's "sensecence." We have periods of togetherness and periods of coming apartness—or transitions. It's a cycle like Spring and Fall and Winter and Summer. We rearrange ourselves, shift gears into the new persona. Adulthood is a time of transformation in an ongoing rhythm of continuity and change, turbulence and calm, including personality change; and transitions occur several times throughout a life span. There has been a dawning awareness about midlife change at least partially stimulated by writer Gail Sheehy's popular book *Passages*, by the work of developmental psychologists Dr. Daniel Levinson of Yale University, Dr. Bernice Neugarten of the University of Chicago, social psychologist Dr. Marjorie Fiske Lowenthal of the University of California at San Francisco, and others who study midlife.

Midlife change, either of work career or lifestyle, is no longer a sign of an unstable personality. A few years ago even an expression of boredom reflected some kind of alleged neurosis. It used to be thought that the "normal" and "mature" person at the end of his teen years was graduated from school, and found a job—whatever job was available or in a career his parents expected of him, that he stayed in it until retirement, settling down into a stable life pattern, fully adult, with no major crises or developmental changes ahead. The truth is, however, that the life pattern created in early adulthood cannot

The Vision

fulfill or reflect all parts of ourselves. At some point, changes in life design must be made to express these parts.

Midlife begins when we look down the vast territory of the highway of life and say "Doesn't it ever end?" We get up in the morning, get dressed, have breakfast, go to work, have lunch, work some more, commute home, yell at the traffic, get into our jeans, do something usual that night, go to bed, get up, and begin again. And pretty soon we look in the mirror and feel like we're robots, like we're imprisoned in the routines of adulthood. And we don't know where we're going. We're marching through life going through these routines without any great sense of what it's all about, and we feel stuck, and we don't know what to do with ourselves. Midlife is feeling embedded in a world that we're not familiar with.

The midlife crisis is basically the change of assumptions about life. We realize that we're not "there." Whatever rewards we thought would be waiting for us when we achieved what we intended to achieve aren't there. And we wonder what we've been working for. We had a notion and ground some path that was climbing a mountain, but when we got to the top of it we discovered that we didn't want to be there. And the assumption we had about building this wonderful life comes to an abrupt halt. Then

29

FUTURE TERRIFIC

we look at the second half of life, and stare death in the face.

The poet Dante may have suffered a midlife crisis and lost his way searching for direction, as he records in "The Inferno":

"In the middle of the journey of our life I came to myself in a dark wood where the straight was lost. Oh! How hard a thing it is to tell what a wild and rough and stubborn wood that was...."

For others, midlife can call for just choosing the road less traveled, as poet Robert Frost may have experienced.

"Two roads diverged in a wood, and I—I took the one less traveled by, and that has made all the difference."

Midlife may be an ending, a continuation, or a dramatic new beginning provoked by a crisis-turned-opportunity, as described by William James, the father of psychology.

"Most people live, whether physically, intellectually, or morally, in a very restricted circle of their potential being. They make use of a very small portion of their possible consciousness, and of their soul's resources in general,

The Vision

*much like a man who, out of his whole bodily or-
ganism, should get into a habit of using and
moving only his little finger. Great emergen-
cies and crises show us how much greater our
vital resources are than we had supposed."*

So Jonathan the rich man has achieved great
business success and an enormous amount of money;
men's lives are conventionally defined by work. But
this formerly aggressive, active, football team captain and do-er, is becoming more introspective, stock-
taking, looking inside himself more. Neugarten
calls this increased "interiority." Our corporate
executive is facing the crisis of his physical bodily
decline. He notices his body isn't what it was when
he was young, doesn't like what he sees in the
mirror. Dealing realistically with his existence, he
faces the inevitability of his death and realizes his
mortality. At 54 he thinks "I only have 20 more good
years." And taking stock of where he's been he asks
himself "What is it I really want?"

He has been a typical male up to now: domi-
nating, aggressive, independent, problem solving.
He finds he is becoming more dependent and passive. He is more inclined to nurturing behavior,
allowing himself to show his feelings of caring for
others. He wants to develop relationships. He has a
new wholeness, sensitivity, cooperation, integra-
tion, a new world view, planetary awareness, a

31

FUTURE TERRIFIC

spiritual unity or connectedness to the world around him with life everywhere, characteristics in the past more associated with women but now known to be crucial for both genders.

This process for a man may mean turmoil or only minor trouble. For him, it brings turmoil in his marriage, for when he turned to his wife for the intimacy he now knows he wants, he discovered she is unable to give him what he needs at this point in his life. This is a new problem because formerly he was attached mainly to his work and demanded little of her personally. He recalls Robert Browning's poem and wishes he could say to a companionable life partner:

> *"Grow old along with me!*
> *The best is yet to be,*
> *The last of life,*
> *for which the first was made."*

For Mark, the computer engineer, it was also personal turmoil. The trigger situation came when he learned about his mother's cancer. He was 41. His father had died years before and he was not married. Through uninterrupted schooling from college to graduate school, then a managerial position with a leading computer firm, and upward on the corporate ladder, feelings were never part of anything he did. But he couldn't hide from the prospect of his

The Vision

mother's fatal illness. Weeks off from work, confusion, crying, terror. Then back to his job and routines, but in his new loneliness, he quickly found a wife. However he has very little skill in interpersonal relationship. So he asks for books to read, and goes to couple workshops, to become the partner he wants to be.

More surprises. He finds that he wants to be free from his career, not tied to his job. And to be "a starving artist." He's through with technology, with the orderly and dispassionate production of concrete products, wants ambiguity and people instead of things. His work is dull and deadening to him. As he puts it "If I'm up on Friday afternoon, and down on Sunday night, it might be time to change careers." At 43 he tells himself "I still have a chance to change. While I can play with bright pears and juicy apples. Should I?" He feels this is the last chance he has of altering his career. He is not only making a living, but making a life.

He refused to be sentenced to incompleteness forever thinking that one occupational focus will carry him throughout life. Life doesn't work that way. Life continues to dance, working and winding its way into broader and more varied development. Career is just the path we leave behind us as our ever more comprehensive and always active intelligence tells us what we need to do next. "If I'm a perpetual

33

FUTURE TERRIFIC

visionary I can keep my life creative. Keep my maximum juice going for me." His crisis had been an opportunity for change.

Following this dream can be revitalizing for him. Many men who don't have a crisis at 40 lose the vitality they need to continue developing, instead becoming stagnant because they have not listened to their yearnings. This is the develop-or-wither career crisis at midlife. Entertainer George Burns, still active and employed at age 92, told a television interviewer when asked how he attained his vital longevity: "Fall in love with what you do for a living."

Marty the playboy, reappraising himself, seems to be missing order, stability, security. Most of us need to work for money to sustain our lives. But work has other meanings for us. When we work, we have a contributing place in society. When we feel important in our work, our identities are enhanced, and our self-confidence is supported. Work helps us know what we are, and how important we can be. The world of work provides most of us with the best single microcosm of the world where we can test our strengths, get appreciated, find rewards, and grow. Now at 45 our playboy feels he should be rejoicing in the wisdom of his life, but instead he feels a despair at futile past efforts. He isn't married and doesn't have a romantic relationship. His parents have both

The Vision

died and he has no brothers or sisters. During the times when he briefly held a job, he remembers "I told myself that the people I worked with were just the people I worked with. But, when I was being honest with myself, I knew that they were my family." Except for family life, where else do we get the intensity of contact with others that we get at work?

He hadn't finished college and had no conventionally marketable occupational skills. What he was good at was recreation. But when he'd tried jobs directing recreation programs in schools or hospitals, he became restless and didn't like being regimented and meeting time schedules and the paperwork.

Dr. Hudson suggested that he write out a job description about a new fantasy position he would love to have: a job making use of his skills and yet giving him the rewards he wanted. It couldn't just be a pipe dream. He began with a list of his interests and aptitudes and a resume of his qualifications, listing sailing a boat, surfing, water skiing, swimming, playing tennis, an enviable knowledge of opera and most music, a marvelous talent for organizing parties and even for preparing food.

His group excitedly determined that he was ready-made for organizing and managing travel tours! He would have to work independently so that

FUTURE TERRIFIC

he wouldn't feel smothered by rules. He would use his own yacht and charter planes. He would be the perfect host. He could turn his ability to play into working at helping others play. But he thought he had to get a "normal" job to be like the rest of us. The group told him that wasn't so, that ideally work should be play too. That he would be contributing to the quality of our lives with his gift of play.

He was relieved and overjoyed. He would have a job yet! And the order and stability and the co-worker family he wanted.

A midlife switch to passive men and wild women? Midlife theorists say it's not quite that extreme, but you get the idea. In the second half of life both men and women alter how they live and be. Both focus on interpersonal issues and look for intimacy in their marital and other relationships. Women become more assertive, aggressive, determined to extend their lives to work outside of the home, to accomplish projects in the world "out there," away from the nurturing, relationship-maintaining roles. This is the so-called "empty nest" period when the children have left. Men's interest is the opposite, leaning more toward increasing capacities for relationships, friendships, emotional bonds, artistry. Self-assessment and feelings about impending death motivate them.

The Vision

Women's lives conventionally have been defined by the family. Jean, our woman lawyer, married at 30 in the midst of a thriving established career of five years as a successful attorney working with one of the best law firms in sophisticated New York City, she thinks as a single woman she would have been earning "big bucks" in an exhilarating lifestyle now. She would have had a feeling of occupational competence. If she had only known what a great opportunity she had given up! She was really part of the first generation of women to succeed in a man's working world. Like most of these women, she had thrown herself into it in her 20s, and it gave her a rush of excitement and self-esteem. But by the time she was 30 she knew something was missing. She was "burned out" as a career woman. Tired of achieving and competing, tired of the solitary burdens of being self-reliant. She wanted a man to take care of her. She thought she would be safe then. She wouldn't be able to have children for too much longer. Without a man in her life, one Sunday, the loneliest day of the week for her, she decided "I'll be married and having a baby in six months." And she was...marrying someone she scarcely knew. It wasn't a romance. She had viewed this lifestyle differently from the vantage point of age 30 than she did now at 53. She was cleaning house and cooking for a husband and three adult children still living at home. The marriage had stopped being loving years ago, and she

FUTURE TERRIFIC

and her husband led separate lives, made easier by their fifteen room house with seven entrances. After college the children will leave and her life will be empty.

Women have more choices in today's world. The boundaries, the "guide-mes," are disappearing, so we can really do what we want to. We have that kind of mobility now. She wants to run away from home. Thankfully, she has a profession and she thinks she can retrieve some of her previous standing. A trip to New York City to her old workplace, a walk past the full-length mirror that's still there, and she's reminded that she's older. But she also knows that she's wiser. She would do an even better job now, wouldn't she? She could call up every lesson she had learned. She needed some self-assurance, some practice, some rehearsal. She needed to reframe herself for re-entry into her occupation, detach herself from her role of the past 20 years.

Our "aging ingenue," as she calls herself, was in a sense fulfilled; she loved being a wife and mother. Married right out of high school, she had never had paid work outside her home. Even though being a "housewife" may not be fully appreciated as marketable work experience on a resume, home-making and work roles are not mutually exclusive, and she knew she had accumulated a lot of know-how. Always volunteering for some organizational

The Vision

work, she had made contacts with lots of people and had edged herself into a social relationship with the wife of a newspaper editor. Making it known that she could write, she said she would like to have her own column. She got it! With one of the largest papers in Los Angeles. She was on her way, she hoped, to a role in show business.

"Unrealistic," some said, imposing their views of her situation. But she knew herself and her experiences better than anyone else could ever know her. "Unreal" is what one person calls the seemingly impossible thoughts of another person.

She felt it was right for her, and she would follow her feelings. If it didn't work, at least she would have done it her way. With support and an action plan she would do it. She would try for the spot of radio talk show host. Time management would be easy. Her three children had moved many miles away. Her parents had died. She wouldn't have role overload. She would continue being a wife, but wouldn't have to be a daughter, and mothering asked scarcely anything of her. Grandmothering wasn't needed yet. Her husband wanted her to have a go at her new adventure. He didn't feel uprooted from an accustomed life pattern. There was enough constancy and sameness between them for a certain stability. The newness made her more interesting and enriched their time together. As an

FUTURE TERRIFIC

extremely accomplished businessman, he could be part of this with her, helping her understand the world of work.

Entering her senior years, Ann was depressed, feeling she was being thrown away because she was "old." In a year she would leave her job with a pension and health insurance for the rest of her life. She felt stuck, sad, scared, angry that she was being pushed aside, embarassed, insulted. Living alone she would miss her co-workers. Her work time, which had taken up most of her life space, would be replaced by personal time, which could mean that she would be isolated from people and idle. She didn't go farther in school than 8th grade. Being a wife and mother and later a secretary were all she knew. In retirement she would have time on her hands and nothing to do. Her daughters were married and lived in various parts of the country, so mothering and grandmothering was a sometime activity. She wanted to learn, to achieve. To have people around her. To help others.

Having her own business would put her in touch with people, take up her time, and bring in extra money she could use. Typing had been a daily work performance for her, and she had become quite a good typist after thirty years. She could buy a computer and put together a word processing service offered through electronic networking. She

The Vision

would guarantee overnight copy anywhere in the country. Delivery without leaving her home. She decided to try it.

CHAPTER 2

Lifecycle Changes

Lifecycle Changes

CHAPTER 2

Lifecycle Changes

Who am I, as an adult, at this time in my life?
What is my identity, as a person...as a
worker...as a lover...as a spirit?

Where am I going? What is my personal
mission, my vocation, my sense of destiny?
Have I the capacity to commit myself to my
mission, to attach to a sense of purpose in my
life?

Who's going with me? Who are my intimate
others? My mate or lover, my family or
friends? How deeply am I committed to
them, and they to me?

FUTURE TERRIFIC

Why do schools teach us so little about midlife issues? Provide such meager guidance to assist adults in enhancing their lives by understanding their life themes, managing personal and professional change, and inventing the future? When midlife people seek help, they often get advice from people who, themselves, don't understand adults.

Psychologist Carl Jung asked why there are no universities to educate us when we're ready to be educated, which is largely at 40 and older. Jung said that when most of us arrive at 40 for the first time we're able to learn the total human imprint. Because that's when we know the questions we need to be asking, when we're willing to ask the questions about existence, and to listen to the answers.

The jobs we belong to pretty much use us. They're draining us. They are opportunities for growth in some ways. But corporate training programs are not really aimed at adult issues. They largely train people who stay put in the organizations where they are and thrive there. The training is not oriented to what's best for a person. It's aimed at organizational issues—what's best for the organization.

The churches are not cued into adult development in a complete way. The colleges and universities are training centers, and ought to be training

Lifecycle Changes

adults in all ways. But they mostly train youth who are entering the adult world. And they just offer adults degrees for career change and not much in the way of continuing education courses that are personally helpful. Almost all the resources our society accidentally provides for adults are not at the heart of the adult need.

One of the main resources we think should provide training in adult sensibilities is psychotherapy. But psychotherapy does not teach us the maps of change in midlife. And psychotherapists are oriented not toward adult healthy, normal development, but toward pathology hunting and clinical repair. They start with a diagnosis of what's "wrong" even when the client is just a normal, healthy adult. Many of the dysfunctions of adulthood are normal dysfunctions which will eventually produce positive results. They're opportunities for change. Divorce is that when the marriage has been hurting rather than helping. Occupational stress is that. And we should see these as opportunities to change and master change, rather than as psychotherapeutic crises of illnesses.

A diagnosis for a healthy adult should be "Where do you want to go?" "What's your plan?" "How do you want to design your future?" "What's your potential?" "How can I help you get where you're on your way to?" Very different from the

FUTURE TERRIFIC

psychotherapist who tries to find something wrong disabled, diseased, in everyone, and then to treat it with some intervention while staying neutral to the process as an objective intervenor instead of partici-pant helper.

MDI does speak to the human condition in the adult years, guiding people more meaningfully through those years. It's an organization helping middle-aged people become more powerful with themselves. It's a training center where adults can go to get refurbished and remade and launched again. To know how to say goodbye to what's not working. To know how to begin again. A place where adults are not "treated for" or "medicated for." Adults don't go to MDI to take pills. It's a place where adults like these are seen as "normal." Where they can learn to live with the loneliness. Living with "ontic" loneliness is a fundamental responsibility of every adult—the loneliness of being completely separated from everything else that is meaningful to us for a spell. Feeling like a cosmic orphan.

MDI's five-day workshop first provides train-ing or renewal in human competence. Pathseekers have addressed the strengths they bring, the liabili-ties on the down side, and determined what new skills they need in order to be optimal with manag-ing their futures with competence. These specific competencies come later as needed; at this time they

Lifecycle Changes

are shown how to get the education they need to be more who they are and directed down the right paths to learn on their own what they must.

They are taught self-education and self-renewal as a process which they can use for the rest of their lives. They learn how to be self-renewing, how to manage endings and beginnings. They learn to take care of themselves. They don't have to become dependent on psychotherapists or give up control of their lives to others. Through lectures and group experiences, at the end of the five days they have a fairly clear vision of the next few months or years of their lives.

In an adult world, the midlife helper, the intervenor, should be like a coach of a football team or a coach of a violin group, just encouraging people to do their best, to discover ways they might be better. The coach should be a role model, a mentor. We need organizations that are doing this with adults.

We're living 35 years longer than we did at the turn of the century. Every year the percentage of older adults increases. Older adults feel put on the shelf, wasting away, playing golf or occupied with hobbies. So much of what we offer adults is designed to keep them out of the mainstream. We should be retraining them to be the major leaders of

FUTURE TERRIFIC

our society. They are the benefactors, the contributors, the generative resources that can transform our society. But they have to be treated like primary resources and not like something over the hill when they're past 50. They should be seen as incrementally better until they're in their 80s or 90s or even when they're a hundred, depending on their competence, not depending on their age. We should find ways of positioning them at the center of their capabilities as that shifts throughout the life cycle, of benefiting from their accrued wisdom. That's what's called for. Poet George Herbert said:

"And now in age I bud again, after so many deaths I live and write...."

The society that figures out how to do that is going to be the leading society. The organizations that figure out how to do that are going to be the excellent organizations. All this talk about excellence is directly related to the ability of adults to discern their personal missions and be in charge of their own visions and then link their visions with those of the corporations and other institutions they work with, and then excellence will occur. But it doesn't occur through training executives to be better executives, or managers to be quality managers. It requires knowledge of the personal stuff going on in the lives of the workers. Teaching them to be better persons. People are persons first. Then they

Lifecycle Changes

are executives or managers or whatever they do for a living. Teach them to be better persons, and they will be better workers. It is not possible to describe a professional ideal without describing to some extent a good man, a generally superior person. Nineteenth century English philosopher and political economist John Stuart Mill said:

> *"Men are men before they are lawyers or physicians or manufacturers; and if you make them capable and sensible men, they will make themselves capable and sensible lawyers or physicians."*

Psychologist Abraham Maslow described human-oriented institutions generated if both the interests of the person and society's institutions were maximized for the benefit of all. He stressed that healthy people have a need to work, to grow, to achieve, to be worthwhile, and that work is an enjoyable part of life for the person who likes his job and considers it worthwhile. That healthy people have pleasure in being part of a team, working cooperatively with others as part of a well-organized, well-functioning organization. That improved people improve the organization, which improves the people involved, and so on. He said:

> *"The better man and the better group are the causes and the effects of each other, and the*

FUTURE TERRIFIC

better group and the better society are the causes
and effects of each other...."

One of the major areas of learning has to be about the lifecycle of changes. Where are you in the cycle of changes? Somewhere between a stable life design and crisis, attachment and loss, holding on and letting go? From continuity to transition, meaningful connectedness to alienated disconnectedness?

Dr. Hudson talks about life designs and transitions. When we are in a life design, we have the sensation that the life design is our life, that it is us. Inevitably after several years, something inside us or outside us "triggers" a transition. Triggers on the inside may be boredom or restlessness. On the outside are job changes, a transfer or being fired, divorce, a move to a new town, death of a parent, children leaving home, new friendships, career change, retirement, an accident, going back to school as an adult, marriage, sudden bankruptcy, relationship betrayal, travel. And we are in transition. Slowly or suddenly we feel loss, doubt, distrust, lack of meaning, anger, panic, or a yearning for a road not taken.

A life design begins with a vision, a nebulous notion of the most desired future imaginable, followed by a new beginning. Goals, plans, action steps, time lines give substance to our mission and

Lifecycle Changes

we launch activities focused on our target. Visioning, dreaming, is uncensored reaching for the stars. And then we need to define "Which star was it?" "How do I get there?" "What comes first?" And then there's some kind of monitoring or evaluating we do along the way.

Launching is the sustaining of a plan and adapting it to the changing realities of the world. Taking advantage of the new opportunities that the world puts in front of us. Being a strategic planner with our lives. Making it. Knowing how to evaluate our plans and judging whether we are on the trajectory we believe in and adapting them accordingly: getting married, having children, starting a career, publishing a book, and so on. Being on our way.

Triumphantly our reward is at the plateau. A plateau is recognition that you got more or less what you asked for. If we don't make it to the top, or if we make it and then lose it, we slide down the other side of the circle. We sense that we are without a clear future, without spirit.

Decline comes when we start to complain. Complainers don't have dreams, aren't planning, are bored with life, don't know where they're going, don't know how to give up—don't know how to get themselves out of the life structure. Declining is a time of reminiscing, and denying that anything is

53

FUTURE TERRIFIC

wrong. We're in the "Dis's." Disengagement, disillusion, disgust, disenchantment, disappointment, dislocation, disidentification.

Our unconditional endorsement of a life design ends, and our dream is tarnished and dim. If the old dream and life design can be rejuvenated and extended by change such as in job or relationships, we can be renewed. But if the dream and life design die through sudden divorce, job termination, severe accident, loss of significant friend or family, we are no longer anchored, no longer grounded. There are voids, holes, nothingness. No replacement is immediately imaginable or available. The ending is letting go. Letting go means saying "Goodbye," grieving, going through a death in ourselves of something that is not working. The person we were in the life structure is no more. We are, to a great extent, our connectedness, our imbeddedness. But until we let go, we can't begin again.

We're not just giving up a person or a job. We're giving up networks of friends, networks of connections that were us and that are not exactly the same anymore. We no longer define ourselves with our old reference points. "Who am I?" "I am not his wife." "I no longer arrive to greet my office family 9:00 every weekday morning." "I am not needed to cook dinner for my child." "My mother isn't there for our telephone chats." "Who am I?" "I don't

54

Lifecycle Changes

exist." We feel as if we are looking in on a past life we used to be living. Like we are someone we once knew.

The assumptions that we built into "forever" are no longer valid. We're cut off from all that has mattered, all that has justified our existence. When an ending happens, we must unravel our yarn. We have to learn how to do that. How to stop pretending we are still there. How to be angry. How to grieve it. How to work through the loss for ourselves. That's a very lonely process. No one can do it for us. Loneliness is missing all the reference points of our life structure, really being severed from the meaning we relied upon in that life structure. It's feeling disoriented, without a sense of meaning, lost, that there is no future, that no one can help us, and we don't know how to help ourselves, and we will never find our way.

And it's not "sick." It's a normal process, a normal state of being at this time in our lives. We don't need to be in intensive psychotherapy. We don't need pharmacological agents to alter our psychological states. We just need to learn to manage feeling disengaged, disillusioned, disgusted, set apart from what made sense. And that's okay. If we read the history of man, we find that that's part of all the great literature. Like Odysseus after the Trojan War who didn't know what to do with himself and spent

FUTURE TERRIFIC

his whole return home going through a life change and feeling totally lost on the journey.

But after a while the loneliness becomes positive solitude. We've successfully removed the other life roles and behaviors and we're alone with the parts of ourselves that are most alive. With the deep stuff in us after we take off the last life design that no longer fits us now. After we mourn the loss and departure, most of us find within us a reservoir of strength that we didn't even know was there. When we're lonely we miss the old life design, and don't know how we'll live without it. We go to the ends of the desert and spend a lot of time wandering and just kind of getting rid of all the clothes and the dreams and everything that went with that. But when we're through, we wouldn't think of going back to that. Solitude is the possession of inner meaning, the realization that we're better off alone, and that it's wonderful to be alone with no life structure giving us roles for our lives. It is a roleless identity. The possession of the self within, instead of things to do to connect with everyone else.

This is a time when we don't do very much. A time of regrouping, of intense inner dialogue. Of consideration of what went wrong and what do we really want to do next. Of major evaluation. When we consider the deepest things in life for us with a minimum of intrusions. For us to know what's

Lifecycle Changes

important and what's not. What's over and what's still going.

After solitude, after we sense what we want to do with ourselves, we're okay without a whole lot of baggage. Eventually our experience in solitude becomes self-healing, renewing, regenerating, rea-wakening, reenergizing revitalizing. We're in the "Re's." This is the beginning of the new beginning, the start of a new venture into the world. We emerge and construct a new life design that fits with who we are now. We have mourned and let go. One of the greatest surprises in life is that we can let go of something we thought we needed to be us, and to still have a great person in there.

There are three steps to reorganizing. We're ready to accept comfort from a few friends, probably new ones, who will validate us as persons. We locate people who can enrich us and welcome them into our lives. We gather information on options for how to proceed with a new life, and begin to experiment with those options, alternative ways of carrying on our lives, like trying on new clothes. We're ready to listen now. "Well, what is it that is my talent?" Put my antennae up and pick up blips. "What are those blips? What should I be listening to and doing?"

Then we have a new vision. An inspiration. A magnetic pull from the top. We fill up our souls and

FUTURE TERRIFIC

our hearts and our lives again. There's a path that we follow and we're sure this is our world.

New beginnings don't happen all at once. We first anticipate what we want. We rehearse in our minds the drama we're writing. We create a script. Scene one, scene two, scene three, with certain players, in a certain place.

And the process is repeated upward around the circle again. We plant and we harvest if all goes our way. And if it doesn't we grieve and plant again. The forest burns and new life springs up from the ashes, life more vigorous than its predecessors. We resurrect ourselves from the dark night of the soul to a new life design and new meanings. And after we've been around the block a few times we know more about what to do with this world.

This is the definition of life. That's it. We are born and we die a thousand times. As a person, as a couple, intimate other, careerist, as one connected to the universe. We need to be able to manage our birthing and dying well. To continue the journey our way. This is the mark of the master in adult years.

That's all there is, and yet it isn't. Every time we go around the circle it has a different meaning to us, even if we change nothing. When we're 30 what we did at 20 has a different meaning. When we're 40

Lifecycle Changes

what we did at 30 has a different meaning. And when we're 50 what we did at 40 has a different meaning, and on and on and on. We keep changing the stories we tell ourselves about our lives.

THE PROCESS OF LIFE

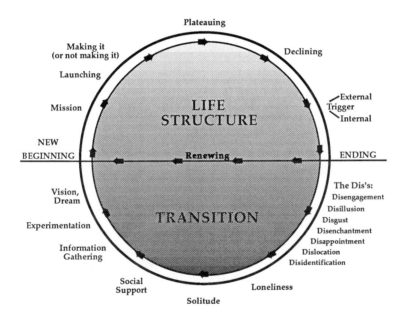

MIDCAREER DEVELOPMENT INSTITUTE

FUTURE TERRIFIC

Locate yourself on the Process of Life diagram. Are you in a satisfying life structure? Have you left one? Are you in transition? Where are you in the circle right now?

Jonathan, the corporate executive rich man, said "Is that all there is? I'm good at business. But as a human being I'm disillusioned with what life means." On the lifecycle of changes he placed himself in a transition, lonely, and beginning to experiment with a new beginning. He had considered retiring from business. But at a healthy 54 with a steady stream of marvelous ideas to keep his business humming and his employees working, he didn't want to give up such a beneficial interest. He had considered divorce but couldn't walk away from a marriage of 30 years without doing all he could to give it a good chance with professional help. So much was happening at such a fast pace with his discovery of himself as a person that he was even more reluctant to alter his life until he knew more about who he was and what he wanted.

The computer engineer, Mark, had passed through an ending—the impending death of his mother, and was launching his first marriage. He was also contemplating a vision of himself as a screenplay writer, a talent he wasn't sure he had. Fatherhood was beckoning, another hope. And personhood was stimulating him, propelling him to behave in all sorts of new ways for him.

60

Lifecycle Changes

The international playboy, Marty was in what was for him a frightening, anxiety-producing, frantic ending. He knew he couldn't go on the way he'd been. Nothing to hold on to. Nothing to cling to for comfort. No substance. He was just a drifter.

Jean, the lawyer, saw herself re-entering the work-world. Information gathering about regaining her law practice. Wasn't as easy as it had been 23 years ago. Many more attorneys out there now. Fewer opportunities. But she was resolved to find a place for herself. She was planning to launch herself in business once again. Determined to do it.

The would-be talk show host, Nancy, didn't see wanting to pick up her childhood attraction to being part of the entertainment business as a tragic ending to anything in her life. Married life had been wonderful and still was. Her life and the people in it would remain as they were. Rather than an ending, it was the addition of a new role, of completing herself, of becoming something she had not been before to make her happier about who she was and what she could accomplish.

Our retiring secretary in her elder years, Ann was making a traumatic change from a busy office job bustling with people to the potential emptiness of daily life alone at home. She was determined not to let that happen. She had handled major transi-

FUTURE TERRIFIC

tions in her life well before, and she was going to do the same with this one. She describes "Late one night, I wrote a letter to my job—a love letter. I said 'I've loved you all these years. You've been so good to me. I've taken care of you. You've taken care of me. My daughters grew up. I've paid off the mortgage on my house. If it hadn't been for you I couldn't have done it. I know the day is coming when I have to say goodbye. When my husband left it hurt so much. And when my daughters married. Parting hurts. I know I have to leave you. I know we have to break up.' I poured it all out. And then I really cried. And since then I don't feel all that attached to my job anymore. Then I started preparing for what I'm going to do after I leave. The day has come when I can walk away and say 'I've given you all I can now, and there's no more to give. I've got to go on to someplace else.'"

Ann knew she must get the someplace else working for her before she left her job, so as she said "Goodbye" she had to have a "Hello." She knew what it was in her work that she prized, and she could create it in some other environment. She would chart it and make it happen. It didn't even have to be work. She needed an environment replacement, not just a project to do. She would be lonely and disappointed if she just did "busywork." She needed people around her. She needed to contribute and to feel important.

CHAPTER 3

Who Am I?

Who Am I?

CHAPTER 3

Who Am I?

Most of us move through life going around the circle of lifecycle changes looking backwards, looking at our past, where we've come from, instead of looking at where we're going, looking forward. We view the future as an echo of the past, and we look into the mirror to see if we are losing it. There's that friendly reminder every morning that we're not quite the same as we were, we're getting older. We cling to the idealization of our youth as the norm to measure our human progress throughout the adult years. The Russian leader Leon Trotsky is quoted as saying:

FUTURE TERRIFIC

"Old age is the most unexpected of all the things that happen to a man."

For much of our lives our bodies are in the process of dying. That's simply the truth. They're in the process of inevitable and predictable deterioration. But we've made much too much of decrements as a definition of what aging is. Aging as we experience it is much more of an incremental reservoir available to us, and it is deepest at our oldest point, assuming we have lucidity, our body is in shape, our organs functional, we have enough money so that money is not our primary worry, and assuming that we have vision and are planning ahead.

French writer Albert Camus said that by the time we're 40 we have the face we deserve. We've etched our own markings. We've become our face. But that's not the way most of us look at it because what we notice is that we're not the way we were. We're not as skinny. We're not as tight. Not as something or other, as if we always should be, as if being that were fulfilling in life. It's merely the way we were. We go through life with this utter nostalgia about the past that's of no use to us. But we don't know that because our sphere of vision is backwards. Until we stumble upon a perspective that says "What I see now at 30 is different than what I saw at 20. And I like this better." Then we establish a new order. But most of us are still going backwards

66

Who Am I?

into our 30s, into our 40s, and noticing what isn't quite the same as it used to be. The ability to turn around and look forward and to design the future, and to seek to become the future, is the most difficult task in the adult years. The charts aren't that clear. There are so many options. It's so complex. It's much easier to notice our deficits, what we no longer can do as well. That we're getting older. We think of aging as getting older instead of getting better.

Your future has already begun with your past. For a terrific new future, you must build on your strengths and overcome your stumbling blocks. Who are you? What has made you what you are? The need at midlife is to assess strengths and weakness and to alter the balance so you can create your finest new steps. Midlife people need to identify these down sides, and then catch up with the talents and abilities they must have and add them to their arsenal of strengths to map out their futures.

Nancy, our prospective entertainer, invested in successfully being a wife, in raising children, and in domestic mastery, but she lacks career skills and economic independence. The corporate executive, Jonathan, knows how to achieve in business but never became acquainted with himself or his wife deeply and personally; now his person is withering, and his marriage never was a union of souls. The computer engineer, Mark, has spent his lifetime

FUTURE TERRIFIC

with ideas and things, and now must learn about feelings and people. Marty the playboy can play but doesn't do much else. Jean, the attorney-turned-housewife, is returning to her profession after having abandoned the life of the career woman, finding that she regretted breaking away from the "fast track" and yielding to the simplistic notion of being safe from all harm and pressure within a marriage. Ann, at 67, has been sole supporter of her children and faithful employee in one job, and now in retirement she must make a new life for herself or be alone and idle.

Everyone is instructed by Dr. Hudson to make a list of his or her strengths, positive attributes, starting each sentence with "I am good at...." Then they do the same for weaknesses, negative attributes, beginning with "I am not good at...." The instructions go on with tasks directed at getting a handle on how to use and improve both facets and then project a different future.

Another way to illuminate our identity is to look at our "peaks" and "valleys." When have we been at our best, and when have we been at our low points? Remembrances of episodes of our lives: a home run for our baseball team at age 10. Grandfather dies when we're 12. First job out of college. Marriage. Divorce. What do these tell us about ourselves? How do we want to be the same in the future? How different?

Who Am I?

Most adults like to talk about strengths more than weaknesses. We like events leading to happiness, and we avoid the dark side of life. For the most part we pretend it doesn't exist. "If I just try hard enough," we may say, "I'll succeed." But trying hard is not enough. We need to understand the resistances, either within us or from outside ourselves, working against us, and to manage them effectively.

The truth is that great leaders calculate their obstacles and threats just as carefully as their strengths and opportunities. We must look at the dark side, the things that might trip up our plan. Through careful strategies we can overcome the boulders on the path that hinder our way so we can create our next chapter in life—to achieve, to be, to love, to play. We want to minimize our disappointments and failures.

What we want from our lives changes with our ages as the years pass. We go through "phases." Our values and commitments are different. Our life structures are based on one or two life issues or "themes." For example, one of our life structures may be based on achievement—wanting a career to go well, weaving a life structure around a job. The sense of identity, then, is a career identity. Every time we go around the circle it is the same circle of visioning, planning, launching, plateauing, declin-

FUTURE TERRIFIC

ing, ending, and visioning again, but it feels like a new ballgame.

Said another way, as our lives mature, our perspective is not the same. We reevaluate, reorganize the importance of our life themes, rearrange our priorities. During a transition we trade off one theme for another that's become more important to us. We can't play them all equally. We have to pick and choose. We favor different themes at different times in our lives.

What's important to us might be encompassed within eight basic life themes: (1) The sense we have of ourselves and knowing who we are and what our impact is on the world around us. (2) Achieving. (3) Passion—that is, energy for what we're doing, feeling alive, vitality—and intimacy with others.. (4) Creativity—building spontaneity into our lives, having humor, being imaginative. It helps us to master change. In the routinization of midlife, creativity is absent. And playfulness. (5) A search for a spiritual aspect of meaning. (6) Contributing or gifting to our planet to leave our world a better place. The older we get, the more we feel we want to leave something of meaning to the world. We want to give to help someone. (7) Daily living maintenance chores. (8) Life-long learning. Through our lives we weave these into an original personal tapestry that is each of us.

70

Who Am I?

The eight themes that compete for our attention want a chunk of us all the time. They are like the eight strings on a guitar; we don't play with all eight strings all the time, but they are there for us. Before we die most of us will have played with all of them to some degree. The question is "Which are the themes to accent now, in what order of importance for your life, and what activities go with these themes?" In a transition, and in the solitude and reconstruction of a new vision, we recalibrate, rearrange which themes are appropriate for our next life structure and the activities that go with them.

Most adults are lopsided, very developed in some ways and not in others. We all have deficits in some area. No one grows up in everything evenly in life. Psychologist Carl Jung talked about the undiscovered self and the several "personas" we have. And there are certain parts of us that emerge at different points in life and yearn to be born. In the course of a lifetime, each of us could be several different characters in a drama. We have the capacity to be different people. There is a certain stability in a personality form, but it's enormously flexible too. We have a great undeveloped potential. We really can do a lot more with ourselves. It can't be done on a weekend or very rapidly, but we can develop different aspects of our personalities.

In young adulthood, typically, we favor achievement in our careers and passion and inti-

FUTURE TERRIFIC

macy as we begin "nesting." How we perform in those areas shapes our feelings about ourselves, our sense of identity. In later adulthood we recalibrate and switch to search for meaning, creativity, daily living maintenance for survival, and social contribution. Playing takes on different forms continuously.

While we're going around the circle in our 20s we're learning some things. We're mainly trying to play around with the world and get away with it. But in our 30s we're wanting more security, more relatedness, and that's a very different way of managing our time. It requires treating the world and ourselves and relationships with more commitment. In our 40s we're rearranging everything, changing our fundamental perspectives. We're not trying to get established in the world. We're not trying to make it. We're trying to figure out how to taste love and a few things well, and to make the journey a quality journey. And that requires very different sensibilities and capacities than making it and all that climbing the mountain of early adulthood. And then in our 50s there's a deepening of that sense of quality. Less is more. And doing a few things well is fulfilling. That proceeds right on into the 60s and 70s, when what's important is contributing to the world, gifting the universe, making the planet a better place in little ways. Like planting trees and flowers and visiting our grandchildren. All of these give us a sense of contributing back for what one has

Who Am I?

received in this long life. It becomes a highly-prized theme.

The dominant theme throughout all the adult years is learning. For example, shifting from maintenance activities as a good wife, supportive of children and family and husband and house, to a sense of self, Nancy is going to know who she is and what to do with her life with or without her husband, with or without her children. She is going to form identity boundaries, a sense of personal power, and go for her destiny. Any time we shift from what has been a major theme such as being a wife to something brand new, we've got to get training. We don't push a button and just pop it up. It's like going back to school, but we're out of school. We're into a learning process. We have to seek out mentors, instructors.

It's the same with the meaning of play. We have to learn later in life how to play in new ways. We don't just ski all the time in later life. We learn ways of laughing, ways of walking on the beach, that are renewing. But they're different from what we used to do. There's the example of an older adult who said "When I was young I'd like to listen to my hi-fi, to 'Beethoven's Fifth' , and I would turn it up as loudly as I could to be sure I heard it all. And now I go to a concert and sit as far back as possible so I can hear it quietly. And I hear it better than I used to hear

FUTURE TERRIFIC

it." That's the difference. We have to learn to hear with our inner selves and not just our ears.

Adulthood does not just happen. We learn to be adults, to carve our paths and choose our priorities, and become the genius we are within us. Learning ought to be a constant dominant feature in our lives so that we become masters of the themes to which we choose to give priority.

The increments as we age are largely in the area of interiority. We sense who we are. We feel a quiet power or passive mastery of the world, instead of always muscular active mastery. Who would want to be young forever? Being old, being "senex," as psychologist Carl Jung called it, is not being weak, it is being wise, conserving, and content. The depth and the power of the old person is in the wisdom, in the memory, in the ability to connect precedent with precedent with precedent with possibility. There's just more in us to consider, a depth that might be useful for anything whether we're commenting on an art form or making a historical observation or planting a rose. Life is more and more of a gift and a celebration.

Aging is your finest asset. Use it. Because as you get older you get a bigger reservoir of experience, a bigger wherewithal to draw from. It allows you to calibrate what's going on more precisely.

Who Am I?

You're able to make more and more sense out of more and more of the world of your experience the older you get. And that prepares you to be a better pilgrim for the future. To be a better venturer for the options that are coming up for you. Aging equals greater resources for managing your future. See it that way.

If you're 40, practice saying "Can't wait 'til I'm 50, because then I'm going to have more power to do thus and so. I'm going to have more insight into myself as I am. I'm going to have my relationships cleared up." Or whatever it is for you. So that you're living into your vision all the time and not bemoaning your past and reminiscing "I wish I could be like I used to be." The truth is you never were that much, and you can become much more. The future orientation is the only way to go anyway. So why not see it as an asset?

You might try to sense the value of the different ages you are with this little game. Gather together people of all ages, separated by decades. Then form them into groups based on the decades in which they were born. People born in the 1930s group together in one part of the room. People born in the 1940s assemble in another part. And the same for the 1950s, 1960s, and so on. Each group then tells the others what their generation has contributed to the world. You are now going to become better

FUTURE TERRIFIC

acquainted with different generations, with people younger and older than you are, hear their dialogue, and integrate it into your sense of destiny. And as you design your future, design it with all the information you can get from the reservoir of our civilization, and not just from your own projection as a person or your own favorite group of people born when you were born. The more you broaden your horizon, the better off you'll be and the more we'll be connected as a society. With great thought in mind, deal with the gifts of many decades as you look at your own line of development. How do you want to be with your themes and your activities as you emerge into your future?

Write down what you do, what your most important activities are, and decipher what themes they represent. This gives you a gyroscope for what you're doing in your life. You will get an inner sense of your values and priorities.

What themes have priority in your life right now? What shapes and proportions do they take on? Are they balanced? Are some overworked, undeveloped, struggling for attention?

Now for a task of great magnitude: how you want your next life structure to be. When you look ahead, what's evolving, bubbling up in you, wanting more attention? That's calling "I'm here. I want

Who Am I?

out. I want you to develop me. Will you go get some learning? Figure it out." For example, your inner self might call out to you "You haven't been very intimate all your life. Now give me a chance." It's begging for you to be intimate with yourself.

What do you want to change? What main theme do you want to increase in your future? What do you want more of in your life in your next life structure? How would you re-order themes? Rank them in order from the most valuable to you to the least important. Which would you like to have top priority? List that as number one. Which would you like to have least priority, so you will be living your life design as a master guiding your path, and not just another wanderer in the universe? List that as number eight. There's no right or wrong way to do this. There are not stages of life you've got to have to be okay except the ones you're choosing and claiming and making happen.

Another way to know who we are is to know what we do in a typical day with our time. To a large degree, we are what we do with our time. Discern how you invest your time, and you will know what you value most and least, what matters to you.

Though we spend a quantity of time doing something, the quality of what we do may not gratify us. We can spend a lot of time doing things and

FUTURE TERRIFIC

never really give our lives away to them. And we can have brief experiences that have profound meaning for us, that can keep our lives glowing for a long time. We may give ourselves to something for only an hour a week, and yet feel recharged from what is to us a fireball of sustenance. What pumps you up?

Henry David Thoreau said: "The mass of men lead lives of quiet desperation."

Poet W.H. Auden told of "The Unknown Citizen" who lived in 1939:

"He was found by the Bureau of Statistics
to be
One against whom there was no official
complaint.
And all the reports on his conduct agree
That, in the modern sense of an old-
fashioned word, he was a saint,
For in everything he did he served the
Greater Community.
Except for the War till the day he retired
He worked in a factory and never got
fired,
But satisfied his employers Fudge Motors
Inc.
Yet he wasn't a scab or odd in his views,
For his Union reports that he paid his
dues,

Who Am I?

*(Our report on his Union shows it was
      sound)*
*And our Social Psychology workers
      found*
*That he was popular with his mates and
      liked a drink.*
*The Press are convinced that he bought a
      paper every day*
*And that his reactions to advertisements
      were normal in every way.*
*Policies taken out in his name prove that
      he was fully insured,*
*And his Health-card shows he was once
      in hospital but left it cured.*
*Both Producers Research and High-
      Grade Living declare*
*He was fully sensible to the advantages
      of the Instalment Plan*
*And had everything necessary to the
      Modern Man,*
*A phonograph, a radio, a car and a
      frigidaire.*
*Our researchers into Public Opinion are
      content*
*That he held the proper opinions for the
      time of year;*
*When there was peace, he was for peace;
      when there was war, he went.*
*He was married and added five children
      to the population,*

FUTURE TERRIFIC

> *Which our Eugenist says was the right*
>> *number for a parent of his gen-*
>> *eration,*
> *And our teachers report that he never*
>> *interfered with their education.*
> *Was he free? Was he happy? The ques-*
>> *tion is absurd:*
> *Had anything been wrong, we should*
>> *certainly have heard."*

Basically we divide our time in six ways: in personal time, being a couple, a part of a family, as a worker, in leisure, and organized in other social groups around various activities. How much of your time is taken up in these six ways?

On a piece of paper, draw a circle. Separate segments of this circle as if you were slicing pieces of a pie, with each segment signifying the amount of time you spend in each of these six ways, describing the roles you play in your life. (Do not include time you are sleeping!)

Happy homemaker Nancy spent most of her time and energy in couple and family, sustaining and developing significant emotional relationships with her husband and children and being there for them as a support in their lives.

Achieving in career, as a worker, that's where Jonathan the rich man spent his time.

80

Who Am I?

Leisure took up mostly all of the Marty's pie.

Mark, the computer engineer, interacted with books, learning and accumulating degrees and developing ideas, and working.

Jean had hidden herself away for years in family as a housekeeper and mother, occupied with the daily living maintenance chores of cooking, cleaning, and caring for children rather than practice her profession as an attorney.

From 9:00 to 5:00 each week day for thirty years, Ann had worked as a secretary in the same job. Now that her children were married and had left her home, there wasn't much to do when she arrived home at night. There also was no one to greet her.

When you consider how your life is spent, do you like it? Do you feel fulfilled? Do you want to decrease a segment? Increase?

How can you create a fair balance? If you are not satisfied with the way you allocate your time, draw another circle, this time with pieces of the pie the size you would ideally like them to be.

CHAPTER 4

*Plans, Action Steps,
Time Lines*

Plans, Action Steps, Time Lines

CHAPTER 4

Plans, Action Steps, Time Lines

The dream comes first. Reality chases after the dream to make it happen. Visioning is picturing new possibilities. Planning implements the vision in the real world. Visioning is dreaming, imaginative, indefinite, motivating, energy releasing. Planning is realistic, logical, definite, factual, and time-driven.

How do we invent the future? The simplest answer is: by simultaneously living visionary lives. A more complicated answer is: by altering our perception of what the future can be and our perception of our capabilities.

FUTURE TERRIFIC

As Henry David Thoreau summed it up in *Walden*:

> *"If one advances confidently in the direction of his dreams, and endeavors to live the life which he has imagined, he will meet with a success unexpected in common hours."*

What is the future? It is not something waiting for us, but something we create. The future is time and piles of potential resources, the not-yet waiting to be given form. And if we don't invent our own future, someone else will fit us into his.

How can we translate our vision into marching orders for every hour of the day? How can we make our next chapter as sure and as definite as possible, the way we want it to be? Plot our drama? Personally translate how the elusive vision is to proceed at any given time and place? Launch our plans, assure ongoing support and networking contacts, and service our plan as we discover new possibilities and realities along the way? When we plan, we take a dream and break it down into goals, action steps, and time lines.

The visioning process is an imaginal excursion. Its purpose is to bring imagination soaring, to find out without any restraints what your best op-

Plans, Action Steps, Time Lines

tions are. It is not to be based on past precedent or constraints of money or energy, but to be conceived just in terms of where we would most like to be, what would motivate us most, what would produce the highest level of energy and excitement and fulfillment for us or for our couple or our corporate team or a nation. A vision is wistful. But it's so visionary in its poetic form that it compels people to do it even though it doesn't say what to do.

Without the vision, the plan is dead. The plan is just a mechanical, managerial notion without motivation, without energy. Without the vision we have a lot of people marching around to change the universe without any sense of how to do what they want to do. We need both. We need a vision that produces the energy and the sense of being pulled toward something we truly believe in; it frees us to shape the future differently than we've been marching in the past. But planning involves taking all the resources and obstacles of our environment seriously so we absolutely can figure out with as much assurance as our mind can give us that we can make it. And if the plan seems dry and dull, return to the vision and fire up, asking yourself "Why am I doing this?" "Why is my launching taking so long?" And then remember the reason, remember the vision, and start over.

FUTURE TERRIFIC

Planning is just the opposite of a vision. Planning is a science and visioning is an art. Planning is being as specific as you know how to to make something happen. Scan the future as businessmen do, being as realistic when you look for obstacles and threats, as you are when looking for opportunities to take advantage of. Invent the schemes to make it happen. And then lock yourself into a time frame— give yourself deadline dates when tasks will be completed. Identify the people who will help you bring your dream to life. How will you learn what you need to enact your plan? Keep reevaluating to be sure you've got the best game plan of all. The compelling vision keeps repeating itself and convincing you of the purpose of your life for a time. And the very explicit plan keeps you a winner.

That's how it works. If you can identify your yearnings and wishes and the things that are bubbling up in your life for the next chapter, and then organize them as a compelling story of the life you most want in the next years, then you can translate that into a plan of action that can get you there, that will define your life for this next period of time.

The journey is from visioning to the plateau. The visioning produces the basic dream and the energy. The planning takes you to the launching. Then there is reaching it and living it in the plateau.

Plans, Action Steps, Time Lines

However, if you happen to be in the "Dis's" or in the solitude and loneliness, what visioning means is a little different. You don't see a great big chapter of your life ahead. There's no way you can. You're still letting go of a chapter that's dysfunctional. The purpose of visioning in that situation is just to see a little bit more—a day, a week, a month, to be able to move slightly forward and not just feel pulled by rubber bands backward as if there's no hope for you. It is the creation of hope in small pieces that you get from visioning. And that's enough.

So if today you get a little vision and a little plan, that's probably all you can do at this point in your life. If, on the other hand, you're ready to take off, then you should map out as much as you can and zoom after it. If you can see light all the way to here, try to plan it. If you're not able to plan it, plan less. And when you reach the end of that plan, prepare the next plan. And you will move. Take as big a "V" vision and a "P" plan as fits you for your life at this time, and celebrate it accordingly.

You will by now have considered the goals that will bring you closer to establishing your vision as a reality. Each goal will fit into one of the following categories: Personal, Couple and Family, Work/Career, Recreation, Friendships, Social Commitment to Benefit Society, or you can create another category you might need.

89

FUTURE TERRIFIC

You have the clues you need. You have a knowledge of who you've been, who you are now, and where you want to be—and you can make that happen. With a sense of your past, your present, and your future, you won't be just wandering around blindfolded. That's no way to go around the circle. So claim your values, your themes, identify the activities which represent these themes for you in your present. You've looked backwards to see how it was in your last design. Articulate your future activities and themes so you can see your sense of destiny, your sense of future, and then you can invent your future.

Now to unfold your grand or small vision. The way to release a vision is not to think very much. Write fast. Just brainstorm. First: Where are you going to be? What are the setting, place, and scenery five years from now, or maybe a month from now? Second: Who are the key players? Who's there with you? Third: What's your story? What's going on? What are you up to? Is it about a new career? Is it some new challenge you're into? New relationships? New leisure? How does your vision affect your personal development, your marriage or non-marriage, your family, your career, leisure, church, society, and anything else? Consider all aspects of your life, weaving them together.

Remember to take your body seriously so that your primary vessel is in shape and is healthy and

Plans, Action Steps, Time Lines

you're taking care of yourself at a high level. A successful plan requires that you understand the acquisition and use of money so you are planning well and money is not a problem that plagues you. Money won't give you happiness, but it gives you freedom from worry about money.

How will your story begin? We all are born and we all die, and what we do in time and space is the issue. We each do something remarkably different. Often we share common experiences, but what we make out of our time and space is unique for each one of us. We do different things. We prize different things. We let go of different things.

Then when you've got your Plan, start out with explicit Action Steps. Write down all of your Action Steps for your Plan for each day. Resolve to not go through any day without following your Action Steps. Not at work, with your mate, or with any other part of your life. Although you've got to carry out your Plan as you have scheduled each day, a good Plan is revised constantly. Never lock yourself into a Plan. Lock into your Vision, but your Plan has to be malleable. You'll get new information and new opportunities. This is a fluid world and you want to be able to change your Plan to maximize newness. But your Action Steps have to be definitive—unless you've got a better Action Step than the one that's on your calendar, you do what you had

91

FUTURE TERRIFIC

scheduled. Write down your goals and action steps, putting each goal on a separate index card.

Place each goal at the top center of its index card. In the upper right hand corner indicate the deadline date when you want and expect this goal to be realized. Then list three Action Steps you will take to lead you from today to the realization of each goal along with a date which will mark its accomplishment.

Keep each step small and easy so you don't overwhelm yourself. Concentrate only on these first three steps. When you complete them you can create more steps.

What do you need to make your plan happen? How will you gather data about your options, about what the world is offering you, and what the obstacles are that work against you? Where will you go to learn what you need to learn? Who are the experts? Call in the troops. Rally the forces—and you've got the skills you need for being future managers of your lives.

Everyone has expertise that may be valuable to someone else. What you've got to learn immediately is to network, both with people who can teach you what you need to know, and also to support you, to be your rooting gallery, your cheerleaders, to

Plans, Action Steps, Time Lines

remind you of what you have resolved to do, and to keep you going and headed in the right direction. Learn to ask and to get and give.

Networking is the way the world works. It's collaborating. Making the world work for you. Knowing how to access information, resources, personal support. Consider everyone you know a resource. Everyone is a link to someone or something else you need.

You need to keep yourself on target. It would be good to have friends who will see you through a new life direction. Tell them what your plans are, make a public announcement of the changes you propose. The more you try to explain yourself to someone else, the more you commit to your own agenda. And ask them for their support. Talk through how you see yourself enacting your plan over and over, about how you're going to do it until you believe it or disbelieve it. Then set a date to re-do your cards.

Program your days to reinforce your plan. Post your action steps up on your bulletin board at home. The night before each day, make an agenda, a schedule of your action steps for the next day. Program yourself to keep yourself on course each day, on a path to the good life you want.

FUTURE TERRIFIC

You are the master of your life. Write a new chapter of your life and act it out to where you want it to be. You can do it.

How did our six pathseekers lay out their dreams in real life? By reaching out, networking, searching for information and consultation.

Marty the playboy, on his 45th birthday, panicked. Time was passing quickly, and he had nothing he could count on. No Routine. No order. No roots. No stability or coherence. He wanted to get up in the morning in a place he recognized, where he'd been living for a while, where the people around him were the same, where he knew people and people knew him. Where there was some predictability, not in a dull way, but in a rewarding way. In a frenzy he had called MDI. He had talked about himself, listened to others talking about themselves, and heard Dr. Hudson's guidance. Now to put into concreteness a way out for him. He began with his work/career. His first goal was to start up his travel tour business. This he broke down into three action steps with more to follow when they were enacted. First he would contact a business similar to the one he wanted to begin, and gather any information he could about the how-tos. Second was setting up an office and hiring a secretary. Third was deciding on a marketing technique for locating customers, such as advertising and direct mailing lists. He would

94

Plans, Action Steps, Time Lines

phone the other model business the day he arrived home after the MDI workshop, set up an office with secretary two weeks later, and begin exploring and assessing marketing strategies in three weeks. Then he would create new goals with three more action steps and deadline dates until his new career was launched and his first tour underway. He took his action steps to his group that afternoon and asked for comments and suggestions, especially from the corporate executive who was expert in forming businesses that made it to the pinnacle. Everyone contributed valuable input. Everyone knew something he didn't know. He gained something from everyone. He was learning the value of networking, of reaching out and asking. He had goals for becoming a couple too. Leisure didn't need to be planned, just reduced, and that would happen when work was added. And when he found a wife.

It was the opposite for Jonathan the rich man. He had to reduce his work, make room for leisure and personal life, and he might have to uncouple. On his first work-goal list he detailed the steps to delegating some of his corporate responsibilities to his employees. Leisure was written into his calendar at definite times each week, and his secretary would not schedule anything else for him at those times. The first action step he would take about his coupling dilemma was marital counseling to help him understand the situation and either come together in

FUTURE TERRIFIC

a better way or divorce. Personal had to evolve as he read books, watched and listened to others, and talked with people to unravel the mysteries of his feelings and identity and relationships. In his new found benevolence, he has decided to start a foundation that will be his legacy to the planet, funding projects for environmental preservation.

Midlife changers need varying types of assistance depending on the causes of the crises. But you may not need personal counseling or psychotherapy for weeks, months, or years; you may be able to learn to take care of yourself in the ways MDI teaches.

Every group member pointed out that our executive had filled out no less than 19 cards with 57 action steps; how was he going to do it all? It was like big business all over again. He had to be alone with himself, unoccupied with anything but himself, to be able to get to his inner being.

He agreed. He didn't know how to just "be." After angrily ripping up several cards he filled out a new one designating "quiet meditation" alone with himself.

Mark, our computer engineer, had to reduce the time and energy spent at his job. To become a more complete person he would yield to the calling to release the artist imprisoned within him. In the

96

Plans, Action Steps, Time Lines

leisure area, which was also neglected, he would start by taking a course in writing a screenplay. That was a giant step for him. Thrilling. Although he was tempted to quit his job and immerse himself in writing, his good sense held him back. He would be cautious and plan this decision carefully. He didn't want to be on the edge, daring, and he wasn't willing to lose. For the moment the writing would be a leisure activity. If he were eventually going to change careers, he would ease into it by writing at night and on weekends. It could always be an avocation if he didn't ditch computers altogether. He and his new wife wanted to have children, and maybe father-hood would temper the mechanization of his work life. His family card must include responsibilities for his mother who was dying from cancer. He felt sandwiched between his wife and his mother, but he enjoyed both, and life wasn't so awful. He would take it slowly and not make any changes he would regret. But he would know where his imagination was leading him, what his energy was being devoted to, and he wouldn't forsake any part of him.

Jean, our lady lawyer, had worked full time for years before she was married, and her identity had been formed as a careerist. At one time she had confidence and responsibility for herself in the marketplace. And she had had economic autonomy. Maybe that's the proper sequence for many women: to have career identity and economic independence

FUTURE TERRIFIC

working first, and then to have a second career of mothering. And then after mothering to go back to work and balance mothering, wifing, householding, and working. But there are no "proper" sequences for any of life's priorities. For Jean, a trip to New York City was a work goal to renew old co-worker friendships and assess her chances at making it again. The same with her law school reunion. She would revive wonderful connections, create a wonderful network. The best way to get a job is to know someone who knows about a job and will recommend you to the employer. She took a review course to update her knowledge. Then she knew she could do it.

She would have to let go of what had been familiar and comforting. But otherwise there wasn't much of a bond to let go of. She plotted her course to finding a divorce attorney, selling her house, sharing the estate with her husband and with children who would need money for college tuition, and she would become independent. She had to have a good financial plan for herself. And medical insurance. She wouldn't want the imponderable and often expensive events of later life to cause impoverishment and dependency. An exercise program and healthy diet would keep her body as vital as she could. She knew now there was no absolute safety in a husband and children, or in anything else, so why not take a risk? She would do without a love connec-

98

Plans, Action Steps, Time Lines

tion. No midlife love life. No matter. At least right now.

Ann's daughter had graduated from a local university, and had told her mother about continuing education courses that could help her with the education she felt she had missed out on. Ann also joined a senior citizen organization and the Gray Panthers. She meets other older people in these groups who have needs, and she finds that she is becoming an adviser: someone's social security check didn't arrive this month; another needs help dealing with a hospital bill Medicare was supposed to pay; another needs a home health aide a few hours a day to assist in caring for her husband who has had a stroke. Ann contributes what she can, and in turn has a new family of friends.

One of her continuing courses was Dr. Hudson's on designing a new future during transitions. That's where she got in touch with the entrepreneur in her. Entrepreneurism is one of the main drives in midlife. To be our own person, in charge of something that makes money, and not caught up in someone else's bureaucracy. She took the five day workshop and realized that she really could put together a word processing service. The resourceful people in her group, many with business experience, generously gave her suggestions, and helped her with detailed plans. Although it took her a year to

FUTURE TERRIFIC

get her business known, she now employs five typists and operates a thriving business in her home. Ann reached the pinnacle of her career at the very time society was telling her to retire. And she's still going. Retirement for her was doing something new in her life that she wasn't able to do earlier.

Get out and meet people. For our budding entertainer, that was the way to find a job. For her career goal, Nancy identified organizations of women she would enjoy spending time with and would develop friendships that might lead to opportunities. Her husband had retired and both were together constantly and thinking "I married forever, but not for lunch." They had not really overdosed, but both would welcome the personal space. Following her action steps and creating more around new developments, she had landed her big chance when one of her organizations asked for a volunteer to write a newsletter column. A part in a play followed, for a charity fund-raiser. More visibility, a new-found social relationship with the wife of a newspaper editor, and an offer to be editor of a newspaper column. And—what's this? A phone call tells me she has just accepted an offer to host a radio talk show! Not in Los Angeles, but nearby. Although she may never make it to the Broadway stage, her life is forever changed. Her future looks terrific!

100

Admissions Form

THE MIDCAREER DEVELOPMENT INSTITUTE
3463 State Street, Suite 520
Santa Barbara, California 93105

805-682-3883

ADMISSIONS FORM

Name _____

Address _____

City _____

State _____ Zip _____

Home Phone _____

Business Phone _____

(See reverse side for available programs)

FUTURE TERRIFIC

Indicate the program in which you are interested:

_____Life Design Program. For planning a new chapter of your life. Cost of a 6-day intensive workshop (offered each month) in Santa Barbara, 12 weekly group sessions in your locale, program materials, and computer network hookup: $2,500.

_____Midcareer Design Program. For planning a new chapter of your career. Cost of a 6-day intensive workshop (offered each month) in Santa Barbara, 12 weekly group sessions in your locale, program materials, and computer network hookup: $2,500.

_____Professional Training Workshop. Cost of a 6-day intensive workshop (offered each month): $1,700.

TO RESERVE A PLACE, MAIL THIS APPLICATION FORM TO MDI. Send a $300 deposit, and we will send you extensive Midcareer/Midlife information to begin your preparation for the program.

Admissions Form

THE MIDCAREER DEVELOPMENT INSTITUTE

3463 State Street, Suite 520
Santa Barbara, California 93105

805-682-3883

ADMISSIONS FORM

Name _____

Address _____

City _____

State _____ Zip _____

Home Phone _____

Business Phone _____

(See reverse side for available programs)

FUTURE TERRIFIC

Indicate the program in which you are interested:

_____Life Design Program. For planning a new chapter of your life. Cost of a 6-day intensive workshop (offered each month) in Santa Barbara, 12 weekly group sessions in your locale, program materials, and computer network hookup: $2,500.

_____Midcareer Design Program. For planning a new chapter of your career. Cost of a 6-day intensive workshop (offered each month) in Santa Barbara, 12 weekly group sessions in your locale, program materials, and computer network hookup: $2,500.

_____Professional Training Workshop. Cost of a 6-day intensive workshop (offered each month): $1,700.

TO RESERVE A PLACE, MAIL THIS APPLICATION FORM TO MDI. Send a $300 deposit, and we will send you extensive Midcareer/Midlife information to begin your preparation for the program.

Admissions Form

THE MIDCAREER DEVELOPMENT INSTITUTE
3463 State Street, Suite 520
Santa Barbara, California 93105

805-682-3883

ADMISSIONS FORM

Name ————————————————

Address————————————————

City————————————————

State———————————— Zip————

Home Phone————————————

Business Phone————————————

(See reverse side for available programs)

FUTURE TERRIFIC

Indicate the program in which you are interested:

_____Life Design Program. For planning a new chapter of your life. Cost of a 6-day intensive workshop (offered each month) in Santa Barbara, 12 weekly group sessions in your locale, program materials, and computer network hookup: $2,500.

_____Midcareer Design Program. For planning a new chapter of your career. Cost of a 6-day intensive workshop (offered each month) in Santa Barbara, 12 weekly group sessions in your locale, program materials, and computer network hookup: $2,500.

_____Professional Training Workshop. Cost of a 6-day intensive workshop (offered each month): $1,700.

TO RESERVE A PLACE, MAIL THIS APPLICATION FORM TO MDI. Send a $300 deposit, and we will send you extensive Midcareer/Midlife information to begin your preparation for the program.

MDI Products and Services Form

THE MIDCAREER DEVELOPMENT INSTITUTE
3463 State Street, Suite 520
Santa Barbara, California 93105

805-682-3883

OTHER MDI PRODUCTS AND SERVICES

_____Professional Assessment Inventory. A complete analysis of your midlife assets in relation to prospective career and life planning options will be mailed to you, and you will be given a personalized report and a one hour interview with an MDI faculty member in your geographic area to plan your next steps. $450.

_____Audio Tapes explaining the 5 MDI Maps for planning the optimal choices of your life and career. Two 60 minute tapes for $25. plus $2.00 postage and handling.

_____*HOW TO GET FROM HERE TO THERE: Daily Readings on Managing Midlife Successfully.* A book of information, references, networks, and compassion. $7.50 plus $2.00 postage and handling.

MDI Products and Services Form

THE MIDCAREER DEVELOPMENT INSTITUTE
3463 State Street, Suite 520
Santa Barbara, California 93105

805-682-3883

OTHER MDI PRODUCTS AND SERVICES

_____Professional Assessment Inventory. A complete analysis of your midlife assets in relation to prospective career and life planning options will be mailed to you, and you will be given a personalized report and a one hour interview with an MDI faculty member in your geographic area to plan your next steps. $450.

_____Audio Tapes explaining the 5 MDI Maps for planning the optimal choices of your life and career. Two 60 minute tapes for $25. plus $2.00 postage and handling.

_____*HOW TO GET FROM HERE TO THERE: Daily Readings on Managing Midlife Successfully.* A book of information, references, networks, and compassion. $7.50 plus $2.00 postage and handling.

Finally...A Helpful Consumer Guide to Psychotherapy

*How To Find A
<u>Good</u>
Psychotherapist:
A Consumer Guide*

By Judi Striano, Ph.D.

If you're shopping for a psychotherapist for the first time or feel your psychotherapist is not helping you, this book is for you. It will teach you to be an educated consumer, looking for the personal qualities and professional skills of a <u>good</u> therapist. This is the <u>FIRST</u> consumer report of helpful and harmful psychotherapists!

It answers these questions:
- Where do I look?
- What qualities are most important?
- Whom can I trust?
- What must I avoid?
- How do psychotherapists help?
- Are professional credentials important?
- How are a psychiatrist, psychologist, and other psychotherapists different?
- How close do we get personally?
- How much do I pay—what's a reasonable fee?
- Where do I report complaints?

"...the most sensible, helpful consumer guide available, offering inspiring quotes about how therapy can help as well as unusually strong consumer testimonials about how it can harm."
        Alex Raksin
        Los Angeles Times Book Review

PROFESSIONAL PRESS
P.O. Box 50343
Santa Barbara, California 93150
(805) 565-1351 phone

Paperback
141 pages
Price $7.95

Finally...A Helpful Consumer Guide to Psychotherapy

How To Find A <u>Good</u> Psychotherapist: A Consumer Guide

By Judi Striano, Ph.D.

If you're shopping for a psychotherapist for the first time or feel your psychotherapist is not helping you, this book is for you. It will teach you to be an educated consumer, looking for the personal qualities and professional skills of a <u>good</u> therapist. This is the <u>FIRST</u> consumer report of helpful and harmful psychotherapists!

It answers these questions:

- Where do I look?
- What qualities are most important?
- Whom can I trust?
- What must I avoid?
- How do psychotherapists help?
- Are professional credentials important?
- How are a psychiatrist, psychologist, and other psychotherapists different?
- How close do we get personally?
- How much do I pay—what's a reasonable fee?
- Where do I report complaints?

"...the most sensible, helpful consumer guide available, offering inspiring quotes about how therapy can help as well as unusually strong consumer testimonials about how it can harm."
                                        Alex Raksin
                                        Los Angeles Times Book Review

PROFESSIONAL PRESS
P.O. Box 50343
Santa Barbara, California 93150
(805) 565-1351 phone

Paperback
141 pages
Price $7.95